HIS GRACE
has brought me
HOME

HIS GRACE
has brought me
HOME

Larry Guenzler

Printed in the United States of America.

ISBN: 978-1-7369703-6-2
Interior artwork: Larry Guenzler
Cover: "Going Home" by Larry Guenzler
Cover & interior design: Rick Lindholtz, for On the Tracks Media

On the Tracks Media LLC
onthetracksmedia.com

10 9 8 7 6 5 4 3 2 1

I wandered so aimless, life filled with sin
I wouldn't let my dear savior in
Then Jesus came like a stranger in the night
Praise the Lord, I saw the light
I saw the light, I saw the light
No more darkness, no more night
Now I'm so happy no sorrow in sight
Praise the Lord, I saw the light

Just like a blind man, I wandered along
Worries and fears I claimed for my own
Then like the blind man that God gave back his sight
Praise the Lord, I saw the light

I saw the light, I saw the light
No more darkness, no more night
Now I'm so happy no sorrow in sight
Praise the Lord, I saw the light

I was a fool to wander and stray
For straight is the gate and narrows the way
Now I have traded the wrong for the right
Praise the Lord, I saw the light

I saw the light, I saw the light
No more darkness, no more night
Now I'm so happy no sorrow in sight
Praise the Lord, I saw the light

I Saw the Light, by Hank Williams
lyrics © Sony/ATV Music Publishing LLC,
Warner Chappell Music, Inc.

TABLE OF CONTENTS

INTRODUCTION

INTRODUCTION

I've lived a fair number of years pondering God's Amazing Grace, and in a non-spiritual world it just doesn't make sense. The FACT that we are given something we in no way deserve – Eternal life with God – is just baffling, but it is reality.

I realize I have lived longer than some and some have certainly lived longer than I. And when I died I am sure I have forgotten far more than I have in my memory bank.

Along with John Newton there are two things I do know though: I am a terrible sinner, and, Jesus Christ is a wonderful Savior.

And that is God's Amazing Grace.

It is His Amazing Grace that took me through to the end of my time on earth, and it is His Amazing Grace that took me to His presence, right to His feet.

As you read this there are certain things you must keep in mind.

First, it is written and presented in three voices:

The voice of my <u>thoughts</u> as I observe what is going on in Glory, presented as centered italic text;

> <u>my</u> voice in conversation with my new friend, presented on the right side;

> and the voice of my conversation partner, my new friend in Glory, presented on the left side.

Why I picked this character I am not sure. To me he has been one of the more colorful characters of the Bible and certainly very vital to the Gospel story.

Also, I do realize that Heaven will not be earth moved up to this wonderful place among the clouds. I do not really expect my own "pad" there, as well as the "town square", stadiums, and concert halls. I am not sure whether I will recognize anyone and do not expect to see our faithful dog, good old Jackson there.

I do expect, though, to see Jesus (oh yes). I do expect there to be such worship and praise like I have never known. I do expect the Glory of God to be on, and around, and in everything – kind of like a foggy day when our whole little world is enveloped by the beautiful atmosphere of the fog. Not that there will be a mysterious fog, but His Glory will envelope us, touching everything. His Glory will be like the fog - that special sphere around us which is all ours alone.

We will have this special Glory of God, all our own and special to ourselves. We will be able to touch Him and He will touch us.

Heaven is special – something we cannot quite comprehend. Heaven is eternal, forever, will never break, or fall apart. Our "toys" break, friendships fail, relationships split, resources dry up and none of it can be fixed, repaired, or renewed.

Holiness, mercy, grace, forgiveness peace, joy, are all defined in Heaven. Worship, praise, and Hallelujah is the language of Heaven.

HOLY, HOLY, HOLY,

LORD GOD ALMIGHTY

MORNING HAS BROKEN

"Morning has broken
Like the first morning,
Blackbird has spoken
Like the first bird.
PRAISE for the singing!
PRAISE for the morning!
PRAISE for them springing
Fresh from the Word!
Sweet the rain's new fall
Sunlit from Heaven,
Like the first dew-fall
On the first grass.
PRAISE for the sweetness
Of the wet garden,
Sprung in completeness
Where His feet pass.
Mine is the sunlight!
Mine is the morning
Born of the one Light
Eden saw play!
PRAISE with elation,
PRAISE every morning,
God's recreation
Of the new day!"

-Eleanor Farjeon

DOORMAN FOR THE KING

An important institution in most large cities is doormen. It has been that way for years and I have an idea it will be for years to come. Doormen have an important job for the business or businesses housed in a particular building. They meet vehicles, welcome guests, give directions, and yes, sometimes open the door for people. Doormen do much more than that though. Often they are the first line of security for the building and ultimately for the businesses. He has power and authority to keep anyone out of the building he wants. The doorman is generally the first person one comes in contact with at the building. Doormen are usually dressed very special because they must look good for the image of the businesses in the building. He is the first impression people get of the building and its inhabitants. Doormen must be the best representation of the facility they can be.

During the Middle Ages, the Lord or master of an estate relied on his door keeper more than any other position in his manor. It was such an important position that it was one of the few positions that was hired by the lord himself. The royalty had more contact with his door keeper than with any other of his employees.

The door keeper was important for a number of reasons. Again, he was the first line of security for his master's house. He could keep any person from seeing his master, and could invite a person for an audience with him. The door keeper met visiting state dignitaries and representatives so he was the first impression that the visitor got of the master and his house.

"...I would rather be a door keeper in the house of my God than dwell in the tents of the wicked." Psalm 84:10b

Can you imagine that, a door keeper for God? What a position that would be. How would that work?

Looking at the responsibility of a royal door keeper, first we must consider security. How does God need security – He is the King of the universe? Indeed, His power is limitless, but He is taking hits on the streets and alleys all over the world. In homes and businesses His name is being profaned and ridiculed every minute. He is being slandered and His credibility is being challenged daily. Way too often we stand by and watch it happen becoming immune to the attacks, and often it is our own actions and indifference that is the culprit. He needs good door keepers. His people are the only ones that can defend His name and character.

The good door keeper must be a good representative of his Master. The door keeper is the <u>only</u> impression that most people have of God. The godly person must be an excellent representation of the King.

The door keeper, very importantly, must invite others in to their Master and King. God offers EVERYTHING to ANYONE who stands before Him.

Door keepers are certainly needed for God's Kingdom. It is more than just looking good and opening a door though. The Holy Door Keeper must defend God's name and His Holy Word. They must be a high and holy representative of the Most High. The Keeper of the Door must invite others to meet the King.

DOOR KEEPERS WANTED.

> Looking at where I am today. I have arrived! I want to go to another scripture. It is one all you have at least heard.

"In my Father's house are many mansions, if it were not so I would have told you…" John 14:2a

There <u>are</u> a lot of mansions He has prepared. A lot of mansions – that is a lot of doors.

LARRY G GUENZLER

FEBRUARY 25 1948

Goals- Strategies - Plans

FRAMED

For me, the most enjoyable part of my work was meeting with and the interaction I had with my customers. I had the opportunity to get into the office of many different people. They were people both very important for the company and they were people who were very important in their own mind. I was able to meet with company owners, presidents, marketing people, secretaries, probably a janitor or two, and some of them all the above.

First thing I did when I entered the office of my contact person was to scour the walls (not literally, I left the comet in my car), to look at pictures, diplomas, certificates, product line information, anything that I could learn about the business and the contact person. At that point I could begin tailoring my presentation to them.

One thing I learned from this quick tour of the office was the real "importance" of my contact and how they would fit into the sales process. I did that by checking the name on the certificates, and diplomas, and by who was in the pictures.

Another thing I learned was stuff about the company – products, longevity, size, objectives, and maybe even a little about my competition.

A top priority to see was usually nicely framed, sometimes on the wall, sometimes sitting on the contacts desk. Wherever it was it was very visible to both office visitor and office holder. This valuable document was the "goals, objectives, and business plan" of both business and personal. This document tells everyone about the health, ambition and integrity of both business and contact, not to mention the real "importance" of the person for the company. Most companies survive by following their goals, objectives, and business plans.

Personal goals are very important also. They are a life road map of sorts, and give us a direction to shoot at. Sometime they are written down and sometime they are top of mind. Sometime they are static, and sometimes changing due to circumstances. Survival can depend on our goals, and objectives, and plans, too often learned after the fact, and too late.

As Christians it is essential that we prayerfully ponder our goals and plans. Too often our high and grand goals are a bit askew when we compare them with what God's goals and plans for us are. Our goals just do not stack up sometime. We often discover that His plan and goals for us are much higher, and the reward as well.

So here I am. Wow, those gates are really pearl. Gee, this is really wonderful – so beautiful. If I didn't know better I would think I was back in Lynden, with the manicured lawns in length, texture, and hue. Funny thing is there is no one working on these lawns. Oh, and look at that ball diamond. This is going to be great.

Look at all the people milling around. I'm not sure if I really recognize anyone… oh, I'll bet that's Methuselah. At least he looks a thousand years old.
I think that's our old dog Jackson –
following his nose down the street.
Oh boy, it looks like Adam changed his fig leaf.
So, here I am at my place – my new pad. Wow, this is pretty nice. Jesus said He was going to prepare a place for me – looks like He sure did a fine job.

Hmmm, no doorman.

Well, what am I doing just standing here –

I think I'll go inside.

Nice. It's fully furnished. I can sure tell that Jesus prepared it just for me. It's so me…and it's certainly so Him. The walls are pretty bare. I guess I'll have to get out my paints and start a picture or two. Oh' by the way I wonder if my stuff has arrived yet.
I got a new set of paints just before….

Ah, there is one thing hanging on the big wall – right in the middle - such a beautiful frame around it.
It's done in fancy script. I wonder what it says…

LARRY GUENZLER

February 25, 1948

Goals – Strategies – Plans

>

>

>

Hey wait a minute. This is not at all like my list.

It's full of blank spaces!

If only... how much better off things would have been for me – oh my, and my family, and those around me.

How much more could I have done for Him...if only...

WELCOME
YOU'RE HOME

BECAUSE HE DIED

Most of us, I would guess, have been put in a situation of
going into a space, large or small, full of people we did
not know – some familiar but for the most part strangers.
I think it is a bit scary for most of us. I used to go to
business and church conferences and conventions not
knowing anyone. What an opportunity. That first step
in is a daunting one, but the right juices start flowing and
the right nerves take over and a good profitable time
usually follows.

*I wonder what's up there? It's so bright. It's a square full of
people. I wonder what's going on. Wow! This is gold I'm
walking on. People are just milling about, just visiting – some
in small groups some in large.*

*Cool, this is a networker's paradise. There are so many people.
So, this is what Buckeye Stadium is like on game day. Ah, but
no game today. I need to see if I know anyone. Well, I see a
tall top hat over there. And there's a guy with a cloud going*

before him. Gross! There's this guy next to me with, it looks like honey in his beard – and bugs. It doesn't look like he's washed his face recently. I'll bet he's noisy on a hot summer night.

I guess I'd better keep moving. Wow, all the people. And I know this isn't everyone. Just listen to the chatter, and all the laughter. I wonder if that's what the joy of the Lord is like.

Boy, the crowd is denser (not a condition) the more I walk in here. I wonder what's going on.

It looks like someone up ahead is doing some speaking.
Let me...

	Oh excuse me...

...push my way through the crowd.
Yup, someone's speaking up there.

	Oh, sorry...

There, I can see now. I wonder who it is.
What a beautiful set. He's sitting on a –

	WOW!

-gold chair with a larger one to the left of it. I guess they're thrones. And next to him, well not really next to but all over the place is this – I really don't know how to describe it – little flame. Not on anything - just kind of flitting around in the throne area. Every time the crowd exalts the speaker the flame gets really excited, and dances through the air. I need one more push forward.

	Oh, sorry sir.

*Great, right next to Mr. Honey N Locust. I hope atmospheric
conditions don't cause his beard to go off. That would be
deafening. He seems to know the man speaking pretty well.
He's a little older than the speaker,
but it's almost like they're close relatives.
I like this speaker. He's got a commanding, bold voice, but at
the same time soft and tender – very compelling.
Oh my – sometime it seems like
his voice is coming from the flame.*

*This is great. I wonder if this is a daily thing. I haven't
figured out how to distinguish a day yet, but I wonder.
I need to get a real good look at this guy.*

*He's got a beautiful white robe on. I don't think I've ever seen
a white like that before. It's kind of iridescent. He's clean
shaven and medium length hair. Such a soft but strong face,
with tender welcoming eyes. He's looking right into my eyes
when he talks to us. I want to lock on to that sight.*

He's got sandals on. That's not unusual these days.

Hey, wait a minute, what is that. Oh my.

Let me get a good look at his hands. Oh…

*Such emotion. I've never been so overcome with emotion. I
can't fight back these tears. Oh, I'm down on my knees. When
did that happen?
It's like I was hit in the back of my legs.*

OH MY GOD!

*(Literally)
He's looking straight at me – right into my eyes,
like He can see deep down into my soul.*

I hear Him speak the words:

"WELCOME. YOU'RE HOME!"

Did he really say that - to me?

I can't turn my eyes. Now it's like I can see deep down into
His soul. This isn't really happening, is it?
It's like He and I are one. Don't let this end.
Oh, He's motioning me to stand up. I can't believe this is
happening. As he was welcoming me it is as though
He never stopped talking to everyone else.
It's like He is talking to everyone individually.

Look at those hands – the wounds.
And those feet also – the wounds.
I would have thought those would be healed by now.

> Oh, I'm sorry, sir. I'm just so
> amazed by the reality of His
> wounds.

> Those are the only wounds or scars up
> here. It's so we'll remember what He
> did for us.
>
> That's how we're here, you know.

I can't fight these tears.
I've never known such emotion.
Wow. I thought for the past couple days
that I was here because I died.
I sure had that wrong.

I AM HERE BECAUSE HE DIED!

HEROES

Heroes, for the most part are very good. I think we've all had heroes. They are to be admired, followed, imitated, even named after, and of course some have their name on our backs. Some of my heroes: Brookes Robinson, all-star third baseman with the Baltimore Orioles, Raymond Barry, all-star receiver with the then Baltimore Colts. As far as a musical hero, I always admired Cliff Barrows. As a writer my hero is Calvin Miller, a creative writing master. I admired Abe Lincoln a lot.

The world seems to need heroes. They carry us through the centuries of time.

Wow! That was sure something.
I could do that all day.
(I've got to get off this "day" thing.)
I think I'll step away from the crowd and ponder,
and meditate on all that just happened.

That was powerful and very emotional.

So, I'm walking, I'm walking. I'm skipping, I'm skipping. I'm hopping, I'm hopping. I'm running, I'm running. This is fun. I always wanted to do this on the earth, but was always too self-conscious. I'm skipping. I'm running. I'm hopping. I'm.... Hey! What's this - a ball diamond? Cool stadium. Let's see what the marque says. 'HOME OF THE ANGELS.' Huh... they've got Angels here too, amazing. Oh, there's more, 'STARRING THOMAS DEWEY'.

I wonder if that's the Thomas Dewey I grew up with?

Oh, there's a picture.

No way! I'd recognize him anywhere. Looks just like he did as a kid — orange curly hair, freckles all over. He did fix his teeth though. That's good.

I can't believe he's a star. I remember on the playground we used to hope there were an odd number of guys that showed up. That way just to make the teams even one person wouldn't get picked. It was usually him. But look at this, Tom Dewey a star.

Sorry to say I can't stick around for the game, got to keep moving.

I'm walking... Wow, look at that concert hall. What's the poster say? 'FEATURING DIANE WILTON - SOPRANO SUPREME'.

Oh, there's more, 'TRIED OUT FOR THE ANGELS'.

Come on, someone's messing with me.

'AND MADE IT'.

I remember in Jr. High she was in chorus with me.
At the end of the year the director came to each of us
to ask if we were going to join Chorus in High School
(he was director for both schools).
He came to her and said, "You're not joining
High School Chorus next year, are you?
She was devastated.
And right now, I need to think about
what Jesus was talking about earlier.
I think I will slow my pace a bit
so I can give things better consideration.

I wonder how far I've walked. What's this here?
All right, it's another stadium.
Looks like a track and field stadium.

Hey, the announcer is giving the results
of the over-all events.

"...third, William Davis, second, Billy Cunningham, and over-
all champion Ernie Dawson..."

What? He was from my old neighborhood, too. He was one of
the "dirty gerties" that lived on the other side of the tracks. We
always lost count of the number of kids they had. Ernie was
somewhere in the middle, I think. We lost contact with them
when I was about nine – don't know if they moved or if they
learned to stay away from us, or maybe we decided to terrorize
someone else. Those years that we "communicated" with them,
Ernie wore braces on both legs. He often didn't walk, but just
scooted along on his bottom.

Wow, Ernie Dawson the track champion.

I think my walk needs to take me back – back to the place of
wisdom. I need to go back to the square.

I'm walking. I'm thinking. I'm pondering. I'm crying. I guess I shouldn't have waited til I got here to do this.

I'm thinking about things Jesus said earlier – about heroes. It was something about the least of these, and the first being last and the last first, and how to determine real importance.

If only…

Book of Promises

PROMISES KEPT

People make promises all the time. Some promises are kept – some are not. This is a life truth that we all must learn and carry with us all our life.

Sorry to say, we seem to remember the promises made to us that were unkept much better than those kept and promises we made that are kept better than those unkept.

Regardless, the sincerity of the promise, promises are held out of true faith – faith in the word of the promisor.

Well, I guess I had better head back to the square. This is so exciting seeing the crowd of people, and the cheers and tears of Worship.

Oh look: the "stage" is full of people. Hey, they're kids. Jesus is talking to a bunch of kids.
Let me squeeze in here to hear what He is saying.

I guess I had better listen to Jesus.

It's about faith – child-like faith. He sure seems to have a great time with children. You would think He was one at some time. He seems to understand them so well. Boy, I remember that, except for my children, most kids were either doing something wrong or being punished for doing something wrong.

Oh, maybe I'm thinking of my own childhood.

> Oh, Hi.

There he is again, my new friend with The Beard.

Cool. He nodded back.

> You sure get around.

> You're kinda new here, aren't you?"

I figure I had better say something.

> Yeah, I can't believe I'm here.

I wonder where this conversation's going?

> Well, why? You were a faithful
> servant of the Master. You told others
> of the wonderful grace and mercy of
> the Almighty. You know, there are
> people here because you showed them
> Christ."

> I know, but that's not what I mean.

> So what exactly did you mean?

I didn't know this was going to
turn into a conversation.

Well, I've been waiting all these
years.

I've been looking forward to
actually being here.

Well, a Promise of God is a Promise,
you know. Just like His Truth is the
Truth. Everything He promises
happens. That's why they are called
promises.

I know, but I'm used to broken
promises, it seems like from just
about everybody.

You're here now.

He sure seems like a man of few words.

So, what has He promised and not
fulfilled?

Well... uhh... Let's see...

I guess now I'm the man of few words.

You must realize you threw yourself
into His arms because He was
trustworthy. Right?

Sure, I just...

25

You staked your life on His promises. You knew He was a man of His word. Why else did you commit to Him and follow?

Now that you put it that way...

Let me show you some of the biggest promises you ever saw. You tell me if they were fulfilled or not.

Okay.

He said that He would die – He did.

True.

He said He would rise from the dead three days later, didn't He? He did.

He pauses. Should I say something?

He said He would be seated at the right hand of the Father. Did you see that other Throne?

Sure did.

What about His promise to prepare a place for us – look around. And don't forget His promise to return to gather His saints one day.

Well, what about me - I'm here now?

I know, He came and got you early.
How's that make you feel – special?

Special? I feel special all right.

Look around you – the people, the
worship, and the joy – all of this.

Uh huh.

All of this, which we call Glory or
Heaven, is truly the realization of
promises of the Father of the universe
because He loves us. He always did
and always will.

There's a new name written down in glory

And it's mine, oh yes it's mine

And the white-robed angels sing the story

SO, WHAT'S NEW?

Do you like your name? I think I do. There are names I am sure I would rather not have – George (no offense George, it just seems like everyone is a George. They were when I was a kid), Alfred, Gomer, just to name a few. I am sure also that people with those names would not like to be saddled with a name like Larry also.

Actually, "Larry" means "crowned", as in crowned with laurel which was the prize for winning an athletic event.

Yeah, I am sure I like my name – Larry.

Say, do you want to take a walk?

I think it would be safe to walk with "The Beard".

Sure. Lead the way.

Okay. This way, I guess.

I suppose this means I have to find something to talk...

So, do you like your new crown?

> Yeah. Sure do. What's it for? I see
> everyone has one, and each one is
> a little different.

It's for being faithful, no matter what
we went through. It's for fighting the
good fight, for finishing the course.

It's for aiming for and reaching your
goal of the upward call, and for
persevering through all your trials."

It's your reward for service. That's
why they are all different.

> Oh, you mean... Hey, there's my
> place. It's pretty nice.
> I really like it.
> But what's that?

What's what?

> That... marker, I don't remember
> seeing that before. Hmm, let's see.

It's a white stone.

Huh.

> But that's not my name on it.
> That's someone else's name. What

30

gives? Did they give my place to
someone else?

No.
We are each promised a new name
here. It's uniquely ours. It is so
special that it is only known to God.

Whew, that makes me feel better.
But...

You know me as John...

Ahh, so that's why the beard and the bugs.
Wow, this really is John the Baptist.
Sure explains a lot of things.

...He knows me by a different name.

Why is that?

Well let's go back a bit.

I'm beginning to like this new name thing.

His name is above all other names.
There was no other name like it, right?

Yes.

At one point, it was considered too
holy to even breathe it.

It healed people. It made kings and
rulers tremble. "It controlled the
universe...

Sure did.

We are here because we lifted that
very special and holy name up in
what we did and where we were.

His name was special to us; otherwise,
we would not have called upon it.

Oh, yes.

We are special, very special to Him.
That's why He's given us a new and
special name. It gives meaning to our
adoption to Christ.

How many 'Larrys' did you know?
Looking out at all the throngs of people
and the many, many Angels, do you
feel just a little insignificance?

But this name makes you special to a
special God. Go ahead and thank Him.

It's okay, you can cry. Emotions are
allowed here. That's why He put them
in us.

This is a new name, appropriate to who
you are, and yours alone. It's
appropriate to your own special service
of worship.

It is your own special gift from Him.

Wow, a new place, a new friend, a new crown, and a new name.

So, what else is new?

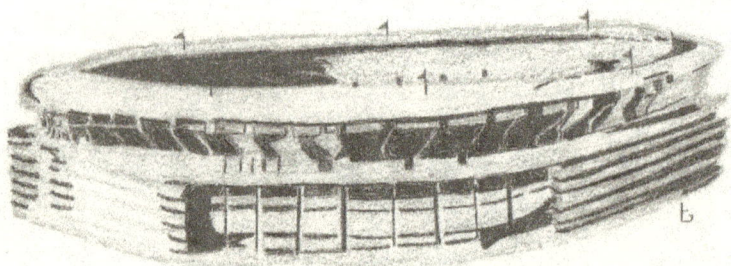

ALL HEAVEN...

We were new to town - moved to Fergus Falls, Minnesota in November, and here it was the middle of January. The big game was just a couple weeks away – the Super Bowl that is. My dilemma was that Fergus Falls was not like Rockford. In Rockford there are fans of many teams, Bears, Packers, Vikings, Rams..., well the list goes on. In Fergus Falls everyone is a Vikings fan.

So...?

So I was a Pittsburgh Steelers fan, and the Steelers were playing the Vikings in the Super Bowl, and friends are good to have, and I know any future friendships may be at stake on that one Sunday in January.

It didn't seem to matter. We were invited to some newly-made friends for dinner and the game (at that time I hadn't told anyone my secret).

The day went well. Good food and a fine football game – for me. Steelers won quite handily.

It was difficult to watch though. Ted moaned through the whole game. So, what do I do? After all we were their guests, and new friends. Do I blow all that with too much exuberance?

Well, I did cheer every time the Steelers scored – silently, deep down inside. I hate to admit it, but I did a great acting job that day. It's amazing what a little self-control will accomplish.

A little later I had to admit everything. Thankfully all was forgiven. The whole incident was actually fodder for some laughter. Things turned out well on a special day with some special friends even though I had to keep my joy and celebrating to myself.

> Hey, let's sit a while on that bench over there and take in more of this splendor, okay?

> Sure. You know, it is never ending.

> I just can't get over this place. Not that I want to either. It's just so beautiful.

> Well, you realize the earth used to be a much more glorious place also. God created a perfect universe – perfect in every way. As you are somewhat speechless about what you take in around you here, it is also hard to

describe the earth at creation and beyond. I know I don't look like a prize creation, but everything He touches is perfect even when to our eyes it isn't so glorious.

So true, I...

It's too bad but it seems like it's part of natural man that the first line of maintenance is to begin to tear down – environment, people, and even righteousness.

Wow, yeah.

Say, is there a stadium around here? I know about the baseball, and track and field stadiums, but there seems to be kind of a background noise everywhere you go that...well, that sounds like we are two blocks from Heinz field on game day no matter where we are.

I think I may know what yo...

Hear that? Sometimes it's louder than others, but it seems like an ongoing thing, I don't know how to describe it, - cheering, maybe.

Ha, I know. Not that it has become common and meaningless, but, I've been listening to that noise for over

two thousand years and it's the
sweetest noise to one's ears.

It is a wonderful noise. It's kinda
soothing, but most of all it creates
an air of celebration. It's kinda like
walking around Pittsburgh on
game day for the Steelers – so
sweet...

What?

Oh, sorry, ha, it's a personal thing.
Really, the more I hear it the more
exciting it becomes.

Well a man, a Doctor, who wrote a
narrative about Jesus' life, and
actually wrote about my birth as well
and was around when my head hit the
floor (although no doctor could have
helped me), wrote about this also.

You mean Luke?

Yes. The shingle outside his little room
read, DR. LUKE – WWJD. I'm not
sure what the WWJD meant.

Oh, I know. It's a heart condition -
spiritual not physical.

Okay, you understand then. Well, in
his narrative, Luke tells us while
telling two stories that 'the angels

38

rejoice over just one sinner who repents'. Do you know what that means?

Yeah, I thi...

It means every time just one single person puts their trust in Jesus, any one person, the angels and all of heaven rejoices.

...oh, I'm sorry, I didn't mean to interrupt. I just get excited about the thought of so much love and concern our Heavenly Father has for each of us.

It is an awesome thought. So, that whole passion that He has for each of us is where His Grace comes from.

It is. Just listen.

Excuse me if I weep; these tears are some of the sweetest liquid you will ever find.

Oh yeah.
Can I cheer too?

Sure. One lost sinner coming into the Kingdom is far more important than any touchdown, any extra point, and for that matter, any game.

Let's do this together...

YEAH!	YEAH!

"... he who has seen me ..."

WHERE IS...?

It drives me crazy when I cannot find something I think I know where it is. I look around and: a) it's the last place I look, b) it was there all the time, or c) it was right out in plain sight and I overlooked it.

When I find it I never know how to feel – its either "Boy am I stupid, it was there all the time, or whew I'm sure glad I found that". Honestly, most of the time it is both the above.

> I think I want to get back to the
> square.

> Are you sure? We haven't walked very
> far.

> I know. I'm glad you came with
> me. It sure is good looking at life so
> differently. You know what I
> mean?

Ha, Ha, Ha. Yes, both our lives now
and in the past.

*Boy, I sure missed a lot on earth. I'm really beginning to realize
what was important, and all that I missed.*

So, what are you thinking about? You
look like you're mulling something over
in your mind.

Well, you give me so much to think
about.

Putting it in earthly terms, it's like I
was looking all over for life and it
was in front of me all the time.
Now I know what faith is all about.

Yes, and the best part is that it's just
beginning. Can you say forever?

Ha. You bet I can.

Can I ask you one more thing?

*It's funny;
I don't even notice his beard and bugs any more.*

Sure, fire away.

We're getting close to the square. I
see all the many, many people and
all the mighty and beautiful Angels,
which we talked about earlier. I see
Jesus, and I think I've figured out
the busy flame, but...

So, what about the flame?

The Holy Spirit, right?

That's right.

Well, I see so many great and
wonderful things, but where is God?

You know, the Father.

Boy that was tough to get out.

I haven't seen Him.

Oh yes, you have… and you will.

Huh?

You've seen His Glory all around you.
You see His brilliance everywhere here.

True, I've never seen anything like
this before. Everything is so bright,
and clear - all without a sun. My
dermatologist will be happy. Both
atmosphere and attitude, everything
makes you just, well, um, just want
to Worship. I don't really know
how to say it, but I think I want to
see God.

Sure does frustrate me,
I can't put certain things into words.

I understand. You just can't describe
what you're feeling. Give it time, it's an

unlimited quantity, you know. It's an
unlimited quantity, and quality.

Yeah, but...

OK. You've seen His holiness, you've
seen His Spirit, you've seen Him in all
these perfect beings, and you've seen
His Son – Jesus, right?

Oh yes, that's another undescribable
thing.

"Give it time."

"So, you've seen Jesus."

True.

Jesus told the Jews in the Temple,
questioning who He was, 'I and the
Father are One'. Then, Jesus told
Thomas,' You believe in the Father
believe also in me', singular. He also
told Thomas, 'If you had known Me
you would have known the Father', also
singular. And He told Philip when
asked for the same thing you're asking,
'Show us the Father', a wonderful
answer, '…he who has seen Me has
seen the Father'. You see, the Father
has always been with you.

But… I want to talk with God.

Oh, you can do that. As I said before, look at this place. You see Him and His glory all around. He's here. He's there. He's all over everywhere. Right?

Right.

You can talk to God anywhere, because He is there. Of course, that's nothing new. We had that opportunity back on earth. He was and is everywhere, especially where His people are.

Wow, that's right.

You know that Jesus's name isn't Jesus, don't you?

What? What do you mean?

And you know that the Holy Spirit's name isn't The Holy Spirit?

Come on, what are you trying to do to me?

No, actually they go by **GOD, THE SON,** and **GOD THE HOLY SPIRIT**, because that's exactly who they are.

Oh, my, that's right. Boy, does that put a different spin on things.

He has assured us that His Spirit inhabits the believers. That makes it really easy to have intimate and holy

communion with Him all the time. You
remember that He said 'Pray without
ceasing.'? Well, there you go.

O God you are so good, You are so
faithful to all generations.

"My Grace covered it all"

WHAT A DAY

As a kid I listened to Gospel quartets and loved the music.
One has stuck with me over the years. I think it was
because of the hope that is showed. WHAT A DAY, was
sung, as I remember by Dad Spear and the Spear Family.

> "...what a day, glorious day that will be.
> What a day that will be,
> When my Jesus I will see.
> And I look upon His face,
> The One saved me by His Grace.
> When He takes me by the hand,
> And leads me to that Promised Land.
> What a day, glorious day that will be."
>
> Jim Hall

Wow, what a day this has been.

Oh? How so? You realize that it has
just begun?

It seems like it's been forever already.

Just wait.

I can hardly.

But back to your question. It was cool to see my new pad and some of the people here, and everything but... ...but I saw Jesus... (sob) ...and...and I looked into His eyes... O man... and He looked into my eyes right down to my soul. (sob) And when He looked... my whole life flashed through my mind ...and I thought, 'what am I doing here.' (sob) And as I was looking into His eyes it was like a great rush of water flowed over me and completely engulfed me... and then...then it turned blood red. And... and through His wonderful piercing eyes He said... (sob) ...'My Grace has covered it all.'

Well, none of us deserves to be here. It's only by His love that...

"Hey! What's that – that brightness coming this way?"

It's Jesus.

Now your day is really going to get interesting.

Oh my! I'd better wipe these tears away. I need to look good.

No need. Those days are over.

Wow, here He is. What do I say?

"Welcome Larry.
You did good. Here, take my hand..."

ANGELS

"And suddenly there was with the angel a multitude of the heavenly host, praising God and saying, 'Glory to God in the highest! And on earth peace, good will toward men'." (Luke 2:13, 14)

"Angels we have heard on high
sweetly singing o'er the plains,
And the mountains in reply,
Echoing their joyous strains.
Gloria in excelsis Deo! Gloria in excelsis Deo! "
"Peace on the earth, good will to men
From Heaven's all gracious King!"
"Come and worship. Come and worship.
Worship Christ, the new born King."

Hey, where're you off to in such a hurry?

Oh, no place in particular, do you want to join me? What's up with you these days?

Well, been doing a lot of thinking.

Ah. anything I need to be worried about?"

No, probably not.

Is this something you need to work out yourself?

Oh, heavens no.

Whoops, sorry. It's just that...well it's just that I left the earth a few weeks before we celebrated the birth of Jesus.

You mean Christmas.

Yes, you're familiar with it then?

I get around, I hear the chatter. I was young, but I was there, remember?"

Sorry, I forget. It seems like we've been together forever. Well I think Christmas is gonna be celebrated on earth pretty soon.

I think you're right. They were shining up the streets the other day.

They do that?

No, you don't need to shine gold.
Christmas is a special day here too.
Without Christ's birth, He could not
have died, so this would be a pretty
quiet and lonely place if that blessed
event had not happened.

Wow, I never thought of that.
So it's Christmas in Heaven and on
earth.

It is. Since everyone is used to
Christmas being at this time, that's
what we go with here.

Great! I love Christmas. I think it's
always been my favorite time of the
year. All the gifts aside, I really like
the festivities of the season. Sorry to
say it's not all that way with all the
gravity people...

The what?

Gravity people."

Why is he looking at me like that?

Oh, that's my new word for all those
people who are still on the earth,
bound by gravity. Of course we've
all defied gravity as we left earth for
this beautifu...

Oh, yes.

Why is he shaking his head?

They all miss so much by celebrating the season instead of the Savior. It's holiday this and holiday that. People send their holiday cards, go to holiday programs before they go on their holiday break. Somewhere the Holy Day, Christmas, got lost.

Yeah, the holiday comes and goes but Jesus is there for them all year long.

I especially like the music at Christmas. I generally like music. It really speaks to my soul like nothing else. I'm so glad God included music in creation.

You're gonna like it here at Christmas time, then. Musak is 24-7 'Heavenly Christmas Anthems'.

Ha, Ha, Ha. I remember working at the airport. Do you know what an air...

Sure do. Saw a 747 go by the other day. Wasn't quite sure where he was going. Ha, Ha.

Well, one Christmas Eve at work on the ramp we were waiting for the last plane to come in. It was a beautiful clear night, with the sky full of stars. Then, there they were on the horizon - four bright lights - one after the other, the last four planes.

Oh, my, what a memory.

I felt a Heavenly arm around my shoulders. I didn't see anyone, but I heard this voice, 'remember the Heavenly Angels announcing my birth singing, '...glory to God in the highest..., on that Christmas Eve so many years ago? '

Thank you, God, for this memory.

Then He reminded me, 'Those airplanes are carrying gifts for and from people all over the world. When those Angels lit up the sky over Bethlehem those many years ago they announced a Gift, the special Gift of Eternal Life all over the earth, the Gift of Peace, Gift of Good Will, the Gift of His Love and Joy'.

Indeed, well put. Thank you for sharing that special memory.

A memory indeed... but it was more.

Look at my eyes, full of tears. It was
Life to me.

God bless you, my son.

(sob)
I've been waiting years to join the
Angels as they sing. (sob)
I'm gonna be singing my praise to
Him in a whole new way. It's gonna
be overwhelming to be kneeling
before Him singing my hosannas to
Him. Oh my, sorry. I need to reflect
on His wonderful plan some more.

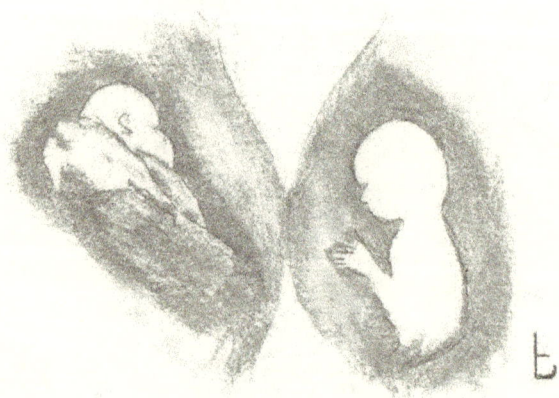

GUESS WHO I BUMPED INTO

I think it's great to "just bump" into someone famous; if not famous, someone special.

I remember Judy Ford, Miss America 1968 – I got to visit with her a few minutes several years ago. Or Leslie Frazier, all-star safety for the Chicago Bears – I got to speak at a Sunday evening church service that he preached at. I also bumped into New York Times best-selling author Calvin Miller at a camp in Bellingham Washington, and had a fun conversation with him.

One person I particularly enjoyed bumping into – Chriss and I had a wonderful conversation with Dr. Thomas McDill, President of the Evangelical Free Church of America one afternoon.

The one who beats it all, though, was bumping into Illinois Congressman Dave Syverson at a men's banquet at our church. When I introduced myself he asked me if I was any relation to Lenn.

"Yes, He's my brother."

"I'll pray for you" he replied.

I appreciate your great Christmas story, but I've got a story for you.

Good, I'd be glad to hear it.

I was bumped into once and I was so excited about it that I jumped for joy; literally jumped for joy when I bumped into Him.

Ha, Ha, let's hear it.

Here goes. Now listen closely. Well, my mom; her name was Elizabeth, was pregnant...

Following you so far.

... with me.

O, my, Ok.

And her cousin was pregnant also.

Hey now, something's going on here. That look on your face makes me wonder.

Let me continue. Her cousin's name was Mary.

Ok, and...?

Well, during their pregnancies Mary
came to visit my mom one day...
...well, they were very excited when
they saw each other. It had been just
very recently that they both knew the
other was pregnant. And...

Oh my, why doesn't he get along with the story?

When Mary walked into the room, like
most women do being huggers, they
embraced each other with an
enthusiastic hug...

Oh my, this is pretty personal.

I didn't think I would be affected like
this in telling it....

...and then it happened.

What happened?

When Mary and my mom hugged their
bellies were pressed pretty close
together and I bumped into The King –
The King of Kings. I don't know if I
can say He was the King yet, but I was
so excited ...

... I just jumped for joy.

Excuse me...it's very emotional...

That's fine. Even my eyes are a bit
moist.

I had just bumped into the King – King Jesus…

"The Angels told our families that this was going to be special, but I don't think any of us knew just how special it was going to be."

I don't know exactly what to say.

"HAIL KING JESUS!

PRAISE GOD!

There's no way that story can be topped, thanks."

"WOW, that's the beginning of how we're all here."

LAST STOP

So, Mr. Bapti…

You can call me John.

Sorry, Thanks. Got time for another story from the airport?

Do I have time?   Ha, ha, ha! Time?
All I've got is time.

Ha, ha, you're right.

You'll catch on. What's up?

Well, ah, this might a get little emotional. I've not told very many people this story. It's emotional for me, but it's good.

Indeed, I'm sure it is.

Well it was one of the safety mantras we were taught at UPS and reminded of continually. It was originally intended for the truck drivers, both over the road and delivery drivers since they made multiple stops every day. Eventually it was intended for all the UPS employees.

OK, following you so far.

That important slogan was, '**Our last stop is the most important stop**', which was very important to me one night.

OK, I think I understand. It meant your shift was over.

Well, kind of. Actually, that 'last stop' was at the end of our night when we turned off our car and were safe at home with our family again.

Oh, wow, that is a wonderful concept for everybody.

Yeah, they began including it for all employees, since we all had an end to our nights.

Yes, I understand.

The sad part was, I knew three or four people who didn't have that last stop.

In fact, one night I almost didn't have that last stop.

REALLY?

Yeah, I was six inches away from being made into sausage when a 6000 pound "can" fell out of an airplane while we were unloading it and it landed six inches from me.

NO KIDDING! Other than the fear factor you came out of it OK didn't you?

I did, although as soon as I got into my car to go home, I began sobbing and couldn't stop. That night I felt very much alone in my little apartment.

I bet...

I'm sorry. I didn't intend the conversation to go this direction. Actually, I didn't tell many people, although the UPS people were somewhat supportive."

You know John, I realized that night that EVERYONE, not just UPS

employees…EVERYONE does
indeed have a last stop.

That's right. Although one night I
didn't have that last stop like you talk
about, with UPS, but I did indeed have
a last stop that night my head hit the
floor.

You bet. God's Word tells us that
there is a time set up that each of us
to die, which is our real last stop.
Then it's judgment time.

Yes, and it's at that judgment where it is
determined where out real last stop will
be – Heaven or Hell.

Wow, how emotional. It's only been
a few days for me. I think my motor
is still warm. The moment I entered
those beautiful Gates I realized My
Last Stop – Glory. And what a
wonderful Home to come home to.

Can I hug you, John… my brother?
I'm finally home.

AMAZING GRACE

So what's so amazing about it?

Well, I can tell you this; I would not be sitting here, at the feet of my Master –THE ALMIGHTY GOD, without it. No way in human terms should I be here. I do not have the means to afford the "trip". Anyway no amount of money will get anyone here. I could not will myself here. If that were the case my face would be as red as a beet from grunting and pushing, which does not get anyone a hairs width toward heaven. Although I claim a little Beaver Cleaver, I am not such a good person to really deserve being here. I think it was Dawson Trotman that said, "…you can say that he or she has a good heart. Our heart is the worst part of us".

No, I do not really deserve Heaven. That is why God's Grace is so amazing – I am in HIS presence whole, righteous, holy and certainly not deserving to be in it. If I got what I deserved I am afraid I would not even get a glimpse of HIS presence, on earth or Heaven.

Death and taxes aside, the #1 certainty is eternal life. Everyone has eternal life. When we breathe our last breath and are just the next job for the landscaping crew at the cemetery, it all does not end. There is a life after we die. We will live forever. **That is our eternal life.** How we spent our eternal life is what is so amazing about grace.

Eternal life for each of us consists of one of two "destinations" – death and Life. Time will not end. We will spend that time either in Eternal Death, dying forever, which is called hell, or spend our forever in the presence of the Almighty God with Eternal Life, which we call Heaven.

When our days on earth are over no one will deserve the latter. We all deserve the former. That is what is so amazing about Grace.

The simple truth about God's Grace is:

We all have sinned - and - the consequence of this sin is death (separation from God) - and - God loves us and sent His Son, Jesus, to die for us. When Jesus died on the cross He took the consequences for OUR sin on Himself - so - We must accept what Jesus did on the cross by faith, and through seeking forgiveness from Him for our sin, turn control and lordship of our life from ourselves to Jesus Christ - and - Know that He is the only one who can save us from our condition.

"For whoever will call on the name of the Lord WILL be saved" Romans 10:13

Call on the name of the Lord? Recognize you have no power in yourself to save yourself. Come to Him through the cross – knowing that He took your sin on Himself at the cross. Commit to Him in faith, knowing that He will save you. Know Him as Savior and Lord.

That's it.

<u>THAT'S WHAT'S SO AMAZING ABOUT GRACE</u>

YOUR GRACE FINDS ME

It's there in the newborn cry
It's there in the light of every sunrise
It's there in the shadows of this light
Your great grace
It's there on the mountain top
It's there in the everyday and the mundane
there in the sorrow and the dancing
Your great grace
From creation to the cross
then from the cross into eternity
Your grace finds me
yes, your grace finds me
It's there on a wedding day
There in the weeping by the graveside
there in the very breath we breathe
Your great grace
Same for the rice and poor
Same for the saint and the sinner
Enough for this whole wide world
Your great grace
Oh, such grace

From the creation to the cross
then from the cross into eternity
Your grace finds me
Yes, your grace finds me
There in the darkest night of the soul
There in the sweetest songs of victory
Your grace finds me
Yes, your grace finds me
Your great grace
Oh, such grace
Your great grace
Oh, such grace
So, I'm breathing in your grace
And I'm breathing out your praise
Forever I'll be breathing in your grace
And I'm breathing out your praise
breathing in your grace
For our God, for our God
Yes your grace finds me
Yes your grace finds me

Jonas Myrin | Matt Redman
© *2013 Atlas Mountain Songs (Admin. by Capitol CMG Publishing)*
Said And Done Music (Admin. by Capitol CMG Publishing)
sixsteps Music (Admin. by Capitol CMG Publishing)
Thankyou Music (Admin. by Capitol CMG Publishing)
worshiptogether.com songs (Admin. by Capitol CMG Publishing)

Also by Larry Guenzler:

OLD SCHOOL FAITH
THAT STILL WORKS TODAY

Devotional From Life
Chapters:

MINNEOTA – LAND OF 10,000   LIFE
NORWEGIANS

IN HIS IMAGE   WONDERFUL WORDS OF LIFE

                                                 BEYOND BARS
SCHOOL DAYS
                                             MORE THAN A GAME
BIRDS OF THE HEAVENS –
FISH OF THE SEA
                                                      TALKIES
GOOD GARDENING
                                                   BLACKHAWK
GOD'S PERFECT DESIGN
                                                      VIETNAM
FOOTBALL GUIDE
                                         BELLINGHAM – 28227
ALL GOOD KIDS LOVE MILK

Available at: amazon.com
                   lulu.com
                   barnesandnoble.com

www.ingramcontent.com/pod-product-compliance
Lightning Source LLC
LaVergne TN
LVHW041233080426
835508LV00011B/1194